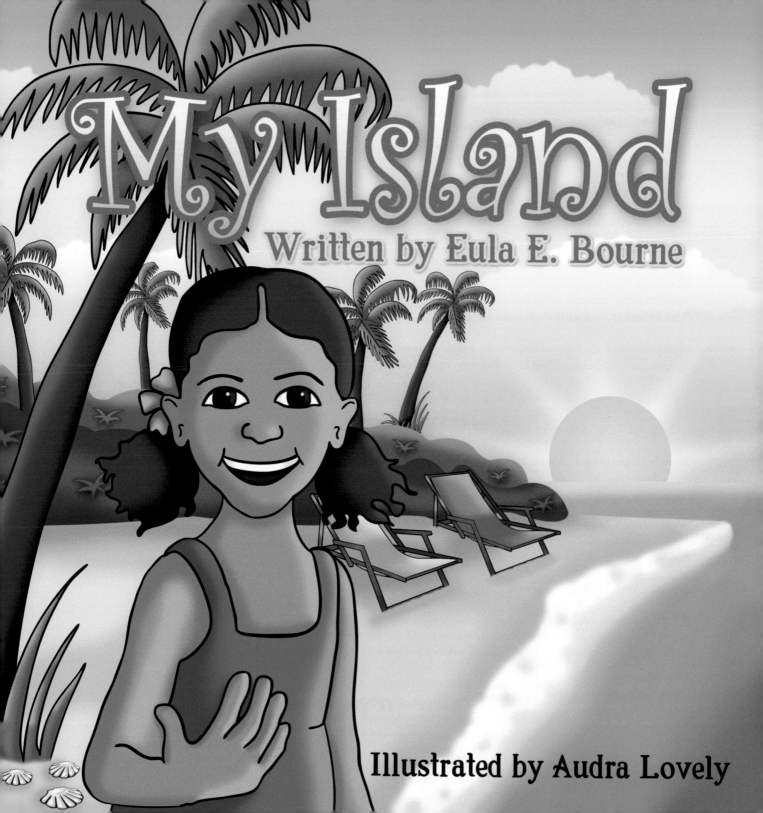

My Island

Written by Eula E. Bourne

Illustrated by Audra Lovely

AuthorHouse™
1663 Liberty Drive
Bloomington, IN 47403
www.authorhouse.com
Phone: 1-800-839-8640

First published by AuthorHouse 09/28/2011

ISBN: 978-1-4567-6898-0 (sc)

Library of Congress Control Number: 2011906241

Printed in the United States of America

Any people depicted in stock imagery provided by Thinkstock are models,
and such images are being used for illustrative purposes only.
Certain stock imagery © Thinkstock.

This book is printed on acid-free paper.

authorHOUSE®

Come with me to my island.
Come, leave your cares behind.
I'll show you how to be content.
To have some peace of mind.

The sea so calm and tranquil!
It's water aqua green!
The beaches stretch for miles and miles!
Creates a wondrous scene!

The palm trees sway in the sunlight,
Of a bright and clear blue sky.
The flamingos stand on one foot,
And squawk as you go by.

6

There's fruit in everybody's yard.
There are cherries and almonds too.
There are hog plums and coconuts,
And mangoes not a few.

We don't have the noise of the city.
The sirens every night,
The endless lines of traffic,
That give us all a fright.

Our island style is quiet.
Our way of life is slow.
We don't always keep a schedule.
We're not always on the go.

There's little time for trouble.
No one has time for strife.
There are other ways of enjoying
Our carefree island life.

We make our own 'excitement'
There are so many things to do.
Like swimming or diving or sailing
Or just lying and 'catching' the view.

12

Our day begins quite early.
We're busy this is true.
But we're never in a hurry.
We'll always find time for you.

The fishermen get up at sunrise.
The farmers they do too.
To feed their growing families.
There's so much work to do.

14

15

A young child runs across the road
As carefree as a lark.
To join her friends who are at play
On a tire swing in the park.

Some children are shooting marbles.
While others climb a tree.
For coconuts are so plentiful.
On our island they're still free.

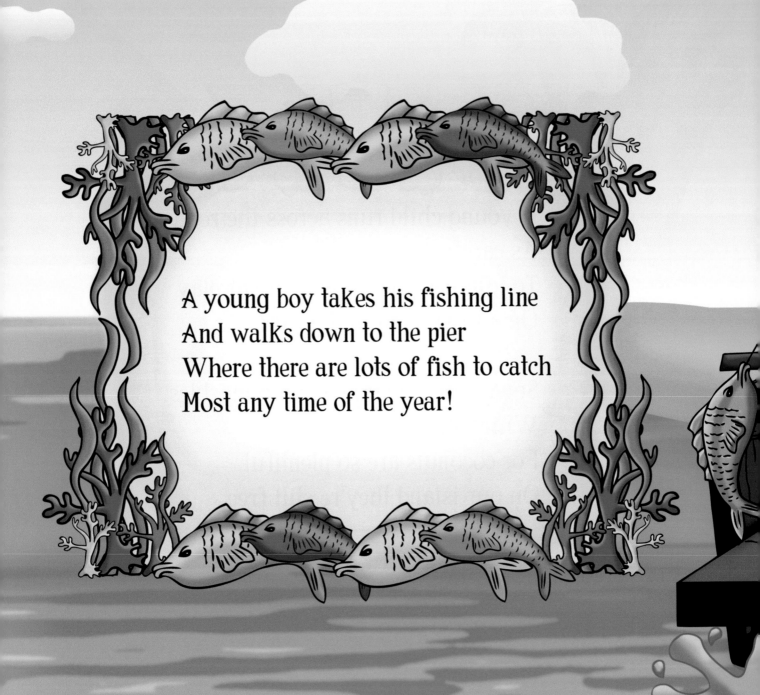

A young boy takes his fishing line
And walks down to the pier
Where there are lots of fish to catch
Most any time of the year!

19

A mother gets her house all cleaned,
And cooks a pot of rice.
If father catches a load of fish,
That would be very nice.

20

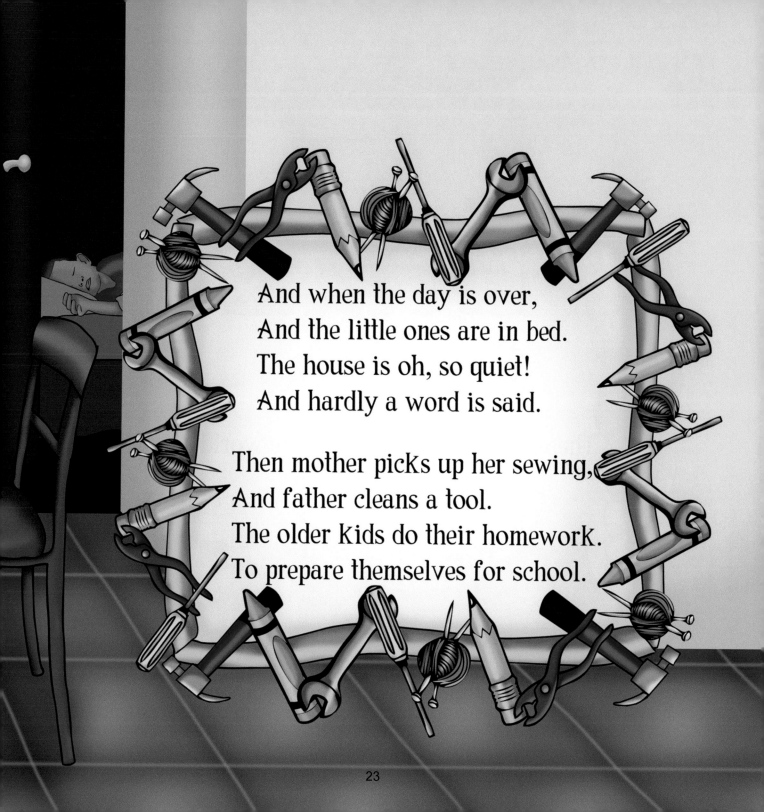

And when the day is over,
And the little ones are in bed.
The house is oh, so quiet!
And hardly a word is said.

Then mother picks up her sewing,
And father cleans a tool.
The older kids do their homework.
To prepare themselves for school.

Our island life is quiet
As you can surely see.
There's no where else in all the world
That I would rather be!

24

Printed in the United States
by Baker & Taylor Publisher Services